COOKING IS A UNIVERSAL LANGUAGE

Published in Italy in November 2021 by
Ciao People srl, Naples,
Via Santa Lucia 97, 80132.

Printed by Amazon.com, Inc. 440 Terry
Avenue North, Seattle, WA 98109, USA.

Interior Photography: Cookist; Istock

"

This is my invariable advice to people: Learn how to cook- try new recipes, learn from your mistakes, be fearless, and above all have fun!

JULIA CHILD

The words of one of the most important cooks in history refer to us: cooking is for many, a daily, necessary and essential act.
At the same time, cooking means much more: it's communication, relationship, culture.

What do we want when we leaf through a recipe book and decide to cook something?
Do we really cook for others with the sole purpose of "feeding them"?Creating a bond between people, showing everyone how simple cooking can be and how you can have fun doing it:
this is what we do on Cookist every day and this is what we want to share with this book.

There are three "keywords":
simplicity, fun, creativity.

The word **simplicity** takes on a completely new meaning: it turns into passion and dedication.
Rediscover the pleasure of spending time in the kitchen, to make those who sit at the table with us feel loved, consolidate bonds, give importance to our passion.
Home cooking and catering find their *trait d'union* in this concept: having **fun**, enjoying the moment, rediscovering oneself and rediscovering others.
Through cooking we can travel, get to know places never before seen, fall in love with distant cultures and understand how they resemble each other much more than you think when it comes to food.
Finally **creativity**, nourished by inventiveness and imagination, is what makes every dish, and every human being, unique in its kind.

And it is precisely to continue to inspire you that we have collected our 50 most loved recipes.
Along with endless tricks: ideas, alternatives and practical advice that will make your relationship with cooking easy, fun and creative.

Francesca Fiore,
editor-in-chief

WHAT'S BOILING IN THE POT

HAVE AN

EGG CELLENT

DAY

6 common myths about eggs you always believed were true

Versatile, easy to cook, and incredibly **nutritious**, eggs are a widely used kitchen staple. However, their popularity has led to rumors and false beliefs over the decades. We debunk six of the most common myths here.

Raw eggs are richer in protein

False. Raw eggs not only do not contain more protein, but they are also dangerous. This is because of the risk of salmonella. That is why many recipes call for pasteurized eggs.

Spots in the yolk are a sign of fertilization

False. Bloodstains in eggs are a sign of ruptured blood vessels that occurred while the egg was forming.

Eggs should be stored in the fridge

This is not always true, but neither is it always false. It depends on storage temperatures. Eggs must not undergo drastic thermal shocks. If you do not know at what temperature the eggs have been stored, it is better to keep them in the fridge.

Eggs can be eaten after the expiry date

Even though eggs do not start going bad on the precise date on the carton, the risks associated with eating expired eggs are extremely serious.

As a general rule, don't eat expired eggs, especially more than 2 to 3 days past the expiry date. You can check if your eggs are safe to eat by using **the water trick** (see page 16).

Brown eggs are more nutritious than white eggs

Colour and shape do not have any influence on eggs' nutritional value. White eggs come from white hens and are no different in flavor or nutritional value from brown ones.

Small eggs are laid by small hens

False. The size of the hens has nothing to do with the size of the eggs. Egg size depends on the chickens' age. Older hens lay slightly bigger eggs.

EGG FRIED
BREAD

This is the perfect way to reuse **stale bread**! It's very quick to make and tastes delicious. So if you fancy something quick and easy, go make some egg bread. Everyone will love the result!

WATCH THE VIDEO

CLOUD OMELET

You only need three ingredients to create an original, **delicious**, **high-protein** main course – ideal for a **light** but **tasty** dinner. If your fridge is almost empty and you're short on time, the cloud omelet is a real lifesaver.

Preparation: **10 Min** / Cooking: **6 Min**   Difficulty: **Low**   Serves: **1 person**

Ingredients

EGGS	2
WATER	2 tbsp
EXTRA VIRGIN OLIVE OIL	
SALT	

A little trick

You can reuse **eggshells** to remove encrusted dirt from pots and pans. Crush or crumble them and sprinkle the powder onto the pan, combining it with a little bit of salt. Leave it for a few minutes, then wipe off with hot water and a sponge.

Preparation

Separate the yolks from the whites and place them in two different bowls. Add a pinch of salt.

Whip the egg whites until stiff, then pour 2 tbsp of water over the yolks and beat them until light and fluffy.

Heat and lightly oil a pan. Pour the egg yolk mixture into it , distribute it well, and cook for a few seconds over medium heat.

Once the yolk mixture has slightly thickened, place the whipped egg whites on top of it and gently flatten out with a spoon. Let it cook for 5 more minutes with the lid on.

Finally, remove from heat and transfer the cloud omelet to a serving dish. Fold it into half-moon , cut it, and serve.

OMELET SANDWICH

This easy, quick, and delicious omelet sandwich can be cooked **straight in a pan** in just a few minutes. It's a clever, hearty option for a **tasty**, last-minute meal.

Preparation: **10 Min** / Cooking: **7-8 Min**   Difficulty: **Low**   Serves: **2 people**

Ingredients

BREAD, TOASTED	2 slices
COOKED HAM OR PROSCIUTTO	4 slices
CHEESE	4 slices
EGGS	3
BUTTER	30 g (2 tbsp)
SALT	
PEPPER	

Preparation

Season the eggs with a pinch of salt and pepper, then beat to combine. Melt the butter in a pan, then pour in the eggs, as you would do for a standard omelet. Place the slices of bread on the omelet and immediately flip it to let the egg soak into the bread. Cook it for 2 minutes .

Gently flip the omelet and line it with the cheese and ham slices. Close the two flaps of the omelet and fold it in two, following the shape and position of the bread (4).

Cook for one more minute, then cut your omelet sandwich in half and serve it immediately.

A little trick

If you love poached eggs but can't cook them according to the traditional recipe, here is a tip for you: gently place the egg in a ziplock bag, close it, and immerse it in water. After a few minutes, your **perfectly poached egg** will be ready.

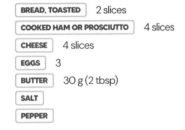

HAM AND EGG BASKETS

This **fast and easy appetizer** is ideal as a main course you can serve as a **quick but tasty dinner**. With only a few ingredients and a muffin cup, you can whip up this recipe in no time.

 Preparation: **10 Min** / Cooking: **20 Min**   Difficulty: **Low**   Serves: **6 people**

Ingredients

EGGS	12
COOKED HAM	12 slices
STRETCHED-CURD CHEESE	100 g (1/2 cup)
PARSLEY	1 sprig
EXTRA VIRGIN OLIVE OIL	
SALT	
PEPPER	

You will also need

A MUFFIN CUP

Preparation

Preheat the oven to 190°C/370°F.

Brush the muffin cup with oil and line it with the ham slices to create your baskets.

Sprinkle with cheese strips and crack one egg into each cup. Season with salt and pepper and bake in a preheated oven for 15–20 minutes.

Now you can remove the baskets from the oven. Let them stand for a few minutes before removing them from the cup and placing them onto a serving dish. Sprinkle with minced parsley and serve.

A little trick

For firmer baskets, you can use **white bread** as a base instead of ham. Cut the bread into small disks and place them in the bottom of the cups.

WATCH THE VIDEO

RED BEET EGGS

This **original**, **tasty** recipe will amaze your guests, both young and old. Thanks to the rich **natural coloring** imparted by the beets, your dish will have a beautiful color. Red beet eggs is a **simple yet surprising dish**, ideal as an appetizer or even as a main course.

 Preparation: **10 Min + 3 hours of rest time** / Cooking: **8 Min**   Difficulty: **Low**   Serves: **4–6 people**

Ingredients

EGGS	6
WHITE WINE VINEGAR	10 ml (1 tbsp)
RED BEET, BOILED	200 g (1 1/2 cups)
LEMON	1
SALT	
PEPPER	

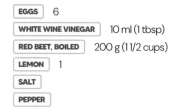

A little trick

Adding lemon to the water weakens the eggshells and makes it **easier to peel them**. If you don't have lemon, you can use vinegar as a substitute.

Preparation

Fill a pot with water and lemon slices. Add in the eggs, bring the water to a boil, then cook the eggs for about 8 minutes. Once cooked, remove the eggs from the pot and run them under cold water, then peel them.

Place the beet in a bowl. Add the white wine vinegar and mix the ingredients with an immersion blender. Pour 200 ml of water into the beet mixture and stir with a spoon.

Put the eggs in the flavored water, cover with cling film, and place in the fridge for at least 3 hours. Drain and dry gently the eggs using a paper towel.

Cut the eggs in half and transfer them to a serving dish. Season with salt and pepper, then serve.

WATCH THE VIDEO

EGG-STUFFED TORTILLA

This clever recipe for a delicious **tortilla filled** with a **tasty omelet** takes just a few minutes to make as the eggs are beaten directly in the pan with the other ingredients.

 Preparation: **10 Min** / Cooking: **10 Min**   Difficulty: **Low**   Serves: **2 people**

Ingredients

- TORTILLAS — 2
- EGGS — 3
- EXTRA VIRGIN OLIVE OIL — 2 tbsp
- CHEDDAR CHEESE, CUT INTO THIN STRIPS
- SALT
- PEPPER
- PAPRIKA
- PARSLEY

Preparation

Brush a frying pan with olive oil and put it on the stove over low heat. Place a tortilla in the pan and break the eggs on top of it (**1**). Stir quickly with a fork (**2**), add the cheese, and season with a pinch of paprika and chopped parsley.

Season with a pinch of salt and pepper and stir to combine the ingredients. Place the second tortilla on top of the eggs (**3**), and cook for a few minutes with the lid on.

Flip the omelet and cook it for a few more minutes. Remove from heat, cut into slices, and serve (**4**).

A little trick

Do you know how to recognize a rotten egg? Put the egg in a glass of water: **if it floats**, it is spoiled; **if it stays in the middle of the glass**, it is safe to eat, but only after cooking. **If the egg sinks to the bottom of the glass, it is fresh.**

WATCH THE VIDEO

DON'T WORRY BE FLUFFY

The perfect rising: 6 secrets to avoid mistakes

If you want to ensure your dough **rises perfectly** each time you bake, make sure you follow these simple tips.

Temperature

For your dough to rise properly, the temperature needs to be around 28°C/82°F. If it is lower, the yeast might not activate. If it is higher, the yeast won't do its job.

Moisture

For the dough to rise, its surface must be moist. The presence of crust, no matter how thin, will hinder the rising process.

Ingredients

Unlike salt, sugar can be combined with yeast to help it rise. Adding a little sugar is essential in both sweet or savory dough. Water also affects the duration of the rising. The ideal temperature is between 25 and 27°C/77 and 80.5°F.

Location

The place where you leave the dough to rise must be neither too humid nor too drafty. It should be somewhere warm but not hot, with a steady temperature.

Timing

Leavening times depend on the type of yeast used, the ingredients, and the kneading. To ensure that the dough is done rising, press it lightly with your fingertip. If it springs back right away and the finger leaves no print, then it is ready for the oven.

Cooking

While cooking, the temperature should be high and steady. To achieve this, you need to preheat your oven. Avoid opening the oven during the early stages of baking to prevent sudden temperature changes.

BANANA FRITTERS

Here's a delicious way to use up your **ripe bananas**.
Fried to golden perfection, these fritters are full of flavor and ready in under an hour from start to finish. So good, you'll want to have them for breakfast, dessert or snack time!

WATCH THE VIDEO

FLUFFY BOW-TIE BRIOCHE

An **original idea** for a simple **family breakfast**, these flaky brioches are as delicious as they are **beautiful**. The recipe is **simple**, and you only need to wait one hour for the dough to rise, then bake them in the oven for 8 to 10 minutes. That's it!

Preparation: **45 Min** / Rising: **An hour and a half** / Cooking: **10 Min** | Difficulty: **Medium** | Serves: **4–6 people**

Ingredients

ALL-PURPOSE FLOUR	350 g (2 ¾ cups)
MILK, WARMED	100 ml (²⁄₅ cup)
WARM WATER	60 ml (¼ cup)
BUTTER	50 g (¼ cup)
GRANULATED SUGAR	40 g (3 tbsp)
DRY YEAST	7 g (½ tbsp)
SALT	6 g (⅓ tbsp)
EGG	1
POWDERED SUGAR	

A little trick

When you combine the yeast with warm water or milk, be careful the liquids **aren't too hot**. If they're too hot, they may **kill the yeast**. Aim for a temperature of around 38–40°C/110–115°F.

Preparation

Place the flour, salt, water, milk, sugar, and egg in a large bowl. Whisk to combine, then add in the yeast. Stir.

Mix in the butter, and knead the dough for a few minutes until it becomes smooth. Shape the dough into a ball, then cover it with cling film and let it rise for about 1 hour.

Cut the dough into balls (**1**) and let them rise for another 30 minutes.

Roll out each ball and then make 7 cuts; make two of these closer together (**2**); intertwine the wide parts one over the other (**3**), and wrap the narrowest strip in the center (**4**).

Arrange the brioches in a pan lined with a sheet of parchment paper, and let them rise for 30 minutes (**5**).  Sprinkle them with powdered sugar (**6**) and bake at 180°C/355°F for 8-10 minutes. Remove them from the oven, let them cool slightly, and serve warm.

20

CONDENSED MILK BRIOCHE

Adding condensed milk to your brioches gives them an **irresistible softness**. **Simple** and **delicious**, once ready, you can **fill** these brioches however you prefer. Try them with cream, jams, or even melted chocolate.

 Preparation: **15 Min** / Rising: **2 h** / Cooking: **40 Min**   Difficulty: **Low**   Serves: **6 people**

Ingredients

ALL-PURPOSE FLOUR	520 g (4 cups)
WARM MILK	240 ml (1 cup)
CONDENSED MILK	80 g (¼ cup)
BUTTER, ROOM TEMPERATURE	50 g (¼ cup)
GRANULATED SUGAR	20 g (1 ½ tbsp)
DRY YEAST	7 g (½ tbsp)
EGG	1
SALT	1 tsp

You will also need

EGG	1
BUTTER	
CONDENSED MILK	

A little trick

To make condensed milk at home, pour 250 milliliters (1 cup) of whole milk in a saucepan. Stir in 250 grams (1 cup) of powdered sugar and 60 grams (3 tbsp) of butter. **Simmer over low heat** for 15-20 minutes, making sure to **stir often**.

Preparation

In a large bowl, combine milk, sugar, condensed milk, egg, and dry yeast; add the flour and salt, then mix using a handheld mixer.

Beat in the butter, then turn the dough out onto a lightly floured work surface. Knead it for 10 minutes or until it becomes smooth. Shape the dough into a ball and transfer it to a bowl. Cover it with a sheet of cling film and let it rise for about 1 hour.

Roll the dough out into a sheet about 1 cm (1/2 inch) thick, then roll it up onto itself (**1**). Cut it into slices (**2**) and transfer them to a loaf pan. Cover and let rise for 1 hour.

Brush the surface with the beaten egg (**3**) and bake in the oven at 180°C/355°F for 20-25 minutes. Remove the brioches from the oven and brush them with condensed milk mixed with a little bit of butter (**4**). Take the brioches out of the mold and serve hot.

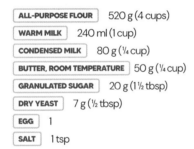

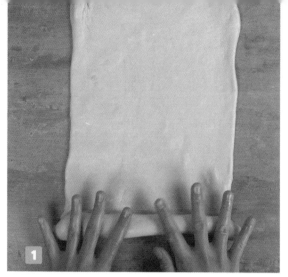

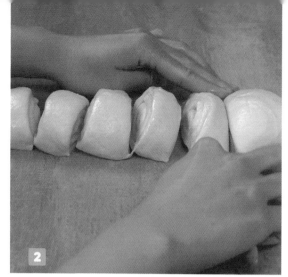

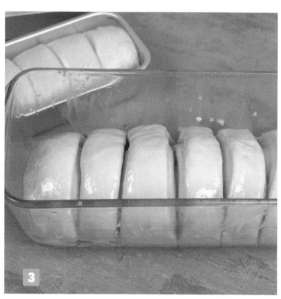

HAZELNUT BRIOCHE LOAF

This **soft**, **moist bread** has a delicious **hazelnut cream filling** and a **crunchy coconut topping** that tastes so good, everyone is sure to love it.
Enjoy it at breakfast or as a a delicious afternoon snack.

Preparation: **30 Min** / Rising: **3 h** / Cooking: **40 Min**   Difficulty: **Easy**   Serves: **4–6 people**

Ingredients

- **ALL-PURPOSE FLOUR** 550 g (4 cups and ½)
- **MILK** 280 ml (1 cup and ⅛)
- **GRANULATED SUGAR** 90 g (½ cup)
- **VEGETABLE OIL** 50 ml (⅕ cup)
- **DRY YEAST** 7 g (½ tbsp)
- **EGG** 1
- **HAZELNUT CREAM**
- **GRATED COCONUT**
- **HONEY**
- **BUTTER**

A little trick

If you only have fresh yeast, you can use it in place of dry yeast. The conversion has a **3:1 ratio**. To convert dry yeast to fresh yeast, multiply the amount of dry yeast by 3.

Preparation

Pour the milk, sugar, vegetable oil, and egg into a bowl, then mix to combine. Sift in the flour and brewer's yeast, and knead thoroughly. Form a ball, transfer the dough to a bowl, cover it with a sheet of cling film, and let it rise for about 2 hours.

After the resting time, roll out the dough into a rectangle and make 3 long cuts, leaving them attached at one end. Spread the hazelnut cream on each strip, close the strips on themselves and then weave them together to form a braid.

Transfer the dough into a 25x10 cm (10x4 inch) greased loaf pan; brush the surface of the loaf with melted butter and let it rest for 1 hour. Bake it in the oven at 180°C/355°F for about 30 minutes.

Remove the brioche from the oven, brush the surface with a layer of honey and decorate with hazelnut cream and grated coconut. Let it rest for 10–15 minutes and then serve.

WATCH THE VIDEO

SPIRAL BRIOCHE WITH HAZELNUT CREAM

This spiral brioche is **soft** as a cloud and **filled with rich hazelnut cream**. This fragrant brioche will delight everyone. Try it for breakfast, with a cup of coffee, or as a snack.

 Preparation: **30 Min** / Rising: **3 h** / Cooking: **40 Min**   Difficulty: **Medium**   Serves: **6–8 people**

Ingredients

for the dough

ALL-PURPOSE FLOUR	350 g (2 ¾ cups)
POWDERED SUGAR	70 g (⅗ cup)
BUTTER	80 g (⅓ cup)
MILK	60 ml (¼ cup)
BAKING POWDER	15 g (1 tbsp)
VANILLA SUGAR	8 g (½ tbsp)
EGGS	2
FINE SALT	5 grams (⅓ tbsp)
EXTRA VIRGIN OLIVE OIL	
EGG YOLK	1

for the chocolate filling

SEMI-SWEET CHOCOLATE	150 grams (1 cup)
MILK	60 milliliters (¼ cup)
VEGETABLE OIL	60 milliliters (¼ cup)
VANILLA SUGAR	8 grams (½ tbsp)

You will also need

CHOPPED WALNUTS OR CHOPPED HAZELNUTS
HONEY

Preparation

In a large bowl, mix the milk, melted butter, vanilla sugar, powdered sugar, brewer's yeast, and eggs; add flour and salt, then knead until the mixture is firm and the ingredients are combined. Shape it into a ball, cover it with a cloth, and let it rise for 2 hours.

In a separate bowl, melt the chocolate with vanilla sugar, oil, and milk.

Roll the dough out into a sheet about ½ cm (1/4 inch) thick; spread the hazelnut cream on one side and then roll up the dough. Make some perpendicular cuts on the smooth dough, wrap it, and form a spiral.

Grease a 26 cm (10 inch) diameter pan with butter. Place the dough in the pan, cover it, and let it rise for an hour.

Brush the surface of the dough with the beaten egg yolk and bake at 180°C/355°F for 30–40 minutes. Remove the brioche from the oven. Brush the surface of the brioche with honey and sprinkle chopped walnuts over the top. Let it cool slightly, then serve.

WATCH THE VIDEO

A little trick

To keep your brioche soft for a long time, don't seal it in a bag. Instead, simply **cover it** with a clean cloth and **store it** in a cool, dry place.

DEEP-FRIED BRIOCHE ROLLS

Soft and **delicious**, you can prepare these brioche rolls with just a few simple ingredients. They are the perfect choice for a **hearty** Sunday breakfast but are also ideal as a **light**, **tasty** snack.

 Preparation: **45 Min** / Rising: **1 h and 30 Min** / Cooking: **12 Min**   Difficulty: **Low**   Serves: **6 people**

Ingredients

ALL-PURPOSE FLOUR	250 g (2 cups)
LUKEWARM MILK	100 ml (½ cup)
BUTTER, ROOM TEMPERATURE	
20 g (1½ tbsp)	
GRANULATED SUGAR	20 g (1½ tbsp)
FRESH YEAST	10 g (¾ tbsp)
EGG	1
SALT	½ tsp
NEUTRAL OIL	

You will also need

SUGAR

A little trick

To fry your brioche rolls perfectly, make sure they are **entirely immersed** in oil at about 170-180°C/335-355°F, and flip them repeatedly until the outside of the whole roll is **golden brown**.

Preparation

Melt the sugar in the warm milk. Add the yeast and mix well. Cover with a lid and let the mixture stand for about ten minutes.

Put the flour in a bowl, add the salt, and mix. Pour in the milk mixture, add the egg, and start kneading. Add the butter and keep kneading until soft and uniform. Wrap the dough in cling film and let rise for about an hour.

After the dough has risen, divide it into 8 pieces and shape them into long strips. Twist them to create rolls, and place them on a sheet of parchment paper. Cover and allow to rest for 30 minutes.

In a large pan, heat the oil. Gently place the rolls in the pan and deep-fry them for 5-6 minutes on each side. When golden brown, remove with a slotted spoon and drain them on kitchen paper. Coat the rolls in sugar, and serve warm.

WATCH THE VIDEO

SOUL CHICKEN

Chicken: mistakes not to make in order to cook it perfectly

Do not wash it

Washing chicken under running water does not get rid of any bacteria present in the meat. It has the opposite effect, spreading the bacteria around your sink and kitchen.

Do not remove the skin

Removing the skin from the chicken before cooking is not a good idea. Skinless chicken can wind up stringy and dry. If you want your meal to be lighter, try keeping the skin on while cooking and remove it before serving.

Do not undercook

Undercooking chicken meat not only results in an unpleasant taste, it is also dangerous. Make sure you heat the pan before cooking the chicken. The meat starts releasing its juices only when it comes in contact with heat.

Do not forget to marinate

Whether you make it with oil, salt, pepper, lemon, milk, or spices, do not forget to marinate your chicken. Marinating chicken makes it tender, succulent, and gives it a rich flavor.

Do not thaw it the wrong way

To be cooked safely, meat can't suffer sudden thermal shocks. This means it can't be transferred directly from the freezer to the pan. Put it in the fridge for at least two hours and then let it rest at room temperature for about 15 minutes before cooking it, or defrost it in the fridge overnight.

Do not crowd the pan

It is important to leave the chicken enough space in the pan when cooking. This ensures it cooks evenly. Do not fill the pan more than necessary. You can also use more than one pan to cook each piece to perfection.

BACON WRAPPED CHICKEN MEATLOAF

Looking for an easy and delightful dinner idea? This meatloaf is the perfect homemade **comfort food**, **easy to make**, cheesy and super **flavorful**. Moist and juicy on the inside and crunchy on the outside, the whole family will love it.

WATCH THE VIDEO

29

FRENCH-STYLE CHICKEN

Are you tired of the same old grilled chicken? Here is a simple recipe to make your chicken incredibly **tender** and **flavorful**. This delicious French-style chicken is a perfect second course that will delight everyone thanks to its **creaminess** and **delicate flavor**.

 Preparation: **30 Min** / Cooking: **25 Min**   Difficulty: **Low**   Serves: **4 people**

Ingredients

BONELESS CHICKEN BREASTS	4
EGGS	2
MILK	100 ml (½ cup)
PARSLEY, MINCED	1 sprig
LEMON	1
DRY WHITE WINE	½ glass
GARLIC CLOVES	2
ALL-PURPOSE FLOUR	
BUTTER	
EXTRA VIRGIN OLIVE OIL	
SALT	
PEPPER	

A little trick

If your sauce is too liquid and you want to obtain a rich and tasty cream, simply pour 1 teaspoon of cornstarch or sifted flour into the pot and stir vigorously.

Preparation

Gently flatten the chicken breasts with a meat tenderizer to even out the thickness. Season the meat with a pinch of salt and pepper **(1)**.

Beat the eggs, milk, salt, and parsley. Dredge the chicken breasts through the egg mixture **(2)**, then dredge them in the flour. Heat oil in a pan and cook the chicken for several minutes, until golden brown and well cooked **(3)**. Remove the meat from the pan and put it aside, keeping it warm.

Melt a knob of butter in the same pan. Saute the garlic with some grated lemon zest. Add the lemon juice and the wine, then simmer until the sauce thickens.

Put the chicken breasts in the pan, season with salt and pepper, and cook for 1 minute. Transfer onto a plate and serve warm.

CRUNCHY CHICKEN THIGHS

Here is an innovative recipe to make your chicken even more **delicious**: crunchy chicken thighs. First, you'll cook the chicken thighs, remove the meat, then mix it with cheese and spices. Then, dip the chicken in panko to give them a satisfying crunch. Thanks to the **super-crunchy** double breading, everyone is sure to love them. Don't be surprised if they disappear quickly!

 Preparation: **45 Min + rest time** / Cooking: **1 h and 50 Min**   Difficulty: **Medium**   Serves: **3 people**

Ingredients

SKINLESS CHICKEN THIGHS	6	
FLOUR	150 g (1 cup)	
STRETCHED-CURD CHEESE	230 g (8 cups)	
CHICKEN BROTH	200 ml (¾ cup)	
PANKO	150 g (1 cup)	
WHITE WINE	100 ml (½ cup)	
GARLIC CLOVES	4	
EGGS	3	
POTATOES, SKIN-ON	3	
ROSEMARY	2 sprigs	
CAYENNE PEPPER	1 tsp	
MUSTARD POWDER	1 tsp	
EXTRA VIRGIN OLIVE OIL		
VEGETABLE OIL	SALT	PEPPER

A little trick

If you want to use frozen chicken thighs, do not **thaw** them at **room temperature**. Instead, put them in the fridge for at least 6 hours up to overnight, then let them stand at room temperature for about ten minutes before cooking.

Preparation

Rub the thighs with salt and pepper. Heat oil in a pan and cook the chicken thighs until they begin to brown (**1**).
Add in the wine and simmer until reduced. Pour the hot broth into the pan, season with rosemary and garlic, then cover with a lid and let cook for 30–40 minutes.

Place the potatoes onto a baking tray, brush them with oil, and season with salt. Wrap them in parchment paper and bake at 200°C/390°F for 60 minutes. Once cooked, remove the tray from the oven, peel the potatoes and mash them while still warm.

Once the thighs have cooked, cut the meat off the bones (**2**). Mince the chicken, and put it in a bowl with the potatoes,

cheese, salt, and pepper. Mix the ingredients, then wrap the chicken mixture around the bones to recreate the thighs, making them more compact with extra cheese. Transfer onto a baking tray (**3**) and let rest in the fridge for one hour.

Dip the chicken in the flour, followed by the egg, then the panko. Fry in oil until golden brown. Drain (**4**) and let them dry on a paper towel before serving.

CHICKEN TACOS

If you are looking for a quick and easy taco recipe, you are in the right place. Here is how to make mouthwatering **fresh** chicken tacos: the perfect choice for a **fast**, **tasty** dinner.

Preparation: **30 Min** / Cooking: **15 Min**   Difficulty: **Low**   Serves: **4 people**

Ingredients

TORTILLAS	8
CHICKEN BREASTS	4
BREADCRUMBS	180 g (1 ¼ cups)
PARSLEY	1 sprig
PARMESAN, GRATED	50 g (¼ cup)
LEMON ZEST	
MIXED SALAD	
EXTRA VIRGIN OLIVE OIL	
SALT	
PEPPER	

Preparation

Cut the tortillas into small disks, fold and arrange them over a grill to make them into taco shells . Cook them in the oven at 190°C/375°F for 5 minutes, or until slightly crispy .

Combine the breadcrumbs, parmesan, parsley, lemon zest, olive oil, and a pinch of salt and pepper in a large shallow bowl. Oil the chicken breasts and dredge them through the mixture **(3)**, pressing them down well so the breadcrumbs stick to the chicken.

Place the breaded chicken on a baking tray lined with parchment paper **(4)** and bake for 10 minutes. In the meantime, toss the mixed salad with oil and salt. When the cutlets are ready, remove them from the oven, let them stand for a few minutes, and then cut them into thick strips. Combine the chicken with the salad and mix well **(5)**. Add the mixture to the tacos shells and serve.

A little trick

Organic chicken tastes best. High-quality, organic chicken breasts should be thick but not too large, with pink meat. If you're using a whole chicken, the maximum weight should be around 2 kg/4 to 5 lbs.

BAKED CHICKEN ROLLS

This fast, easy, yummy chicken recipe is always a winner. Baked chicken rolls are **crispy on the outside** but **creamy** and **soft on the inside** and will delight the whole family. They're a real lifesaver when you need a tasty last-minute meal.

Preparation: **20 Min** / Cooking: **25 Min**   Difficulty: **Low**   Serves: **4 people**

Ingredients

CHICKEN BREASTS	2
COOKED HAM	4 slices
CHEESE	4 slices
EGGS	2
ALL-PURPOSE FLOUR	
PANKO	
EXTRA VIRGIN OLIVE OIL	
SALT	
PEPPER	

Preparation

Heat the oven to 190°C/375°F.

Cut the chicken breasts in half to make 2 slices for each breast. Place on a cutting board and squash gently using a rolling pin to flatten them.

Season the chicken on both sides with a pinch of salt and pepper. Lay the cooked ham slices on the chicken, followed by the cheese slices (**1**), and roll. Flour the rolls, dip them in the beaten eggs, then in the panko.

Transfer the rolls to a baking tray and brush them with a little oil (**2**). Bake the rolls for 25 minutes, or until golden brown. Remove from the oven (**3**) and serve them warm.

A little trick

Here are three tips for cooking your chicken perfectly. **1)** Marinate the chicken breast in olive oil, lemon juice, and salt for about 30 minutes; **2)** remove the chicken from the fridge 10 minutes before cooking; **3)** if the slices are too thick, you can flatten them gently with a meat tenderizer, but be careful not to overdo it.

BREADED CHICKEN STRIPS

You only need chicken, eggs, and your favorite spices to bring this **delicious meal** to the table. The best part is that you can make it in very little time. Breaded chicken strips are a perfect last-minute dish that is ideal as a main course accompanied by salad or served as an appetizer.

 Preparation: **20 Min** / Cooking: **10 Min**   Difficulty: **Low**   Serves: **2 people**

Ingredients

CHICKEN BREASTS	2
EGGS	3
GARLIC CLOVES, MINCED	2
SPICES	2 tbsp
CORNSTARCH	2 tbsp
VEGETABLE OIL	
SALT	

Preparation

Separate the egg yolks from the whites. Cut the chicken into thin strips, and place them in a large bowl. Add the yolks, garlic, spices, salt, and cornstarch, and mix well.

In another bowl, whisk the egg whites until they form stiff peaks. Heat the oil in a large pan. Dip the chicken strips in the egg whites, and fry them in the oil, working in batches if necessary.

When the chicken strips are golden brown and crispy, remove them to drain on paper towels. Season with a pinch of salt and serve warm.

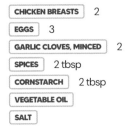

A little trick

If you love grilled chicken, but you find it a little too dry, try **marinating** the meat before you grill it. You can make a simple marinade with olive oil, salt, and lemon juice. Alternatively, you can get creative and play with wine, beer, soy sauce, herbs, and spices.

WATCH THE VIDEO

BREAKING BREAD

How to store bread properly: tips and tricks

Storing fresh bread in the pantry

The easiest way to store fresh bread is to put it in a paper bag. This protects it from moisture. To keep it longer, you can place the paper bag in a plastic one without closing it tightly. Store it in a cool, airy place away from heat sources and direct light. It will last from 2 to 5 days.

Storing bread in the fridge

If you can't find a suitable place for your bread, you can store it in the fridge. Place it in an airtight sealed food container to prevent it from absorbing the smell of other food. Doing this will help your bread last up to 5 days.

Freezing bread

Finally, another way to preserve the freshness of the bread is to freeze it. This works best if it's already sliced. Once portioned, put the bread in a freezer-safe bag or wrap it in a clean cotton cloth. When it's time to thaw it, keep it in the fridge for a few hours, then take it out and leave it at room temperature.

OLIVE
BREADSTICKS

Fluffy, fragrant and so **easy** to make! These sticks are a unique appetizer and they are great served with olive oil or your favorite dips for a party. This recipe will be a hit.

WATCH THE VIDEO

41

QUICK BREAD

Quick bread is a simple recipe that will allow you to prepare a **crunchy on the outside, soft on the inside** bread in no time. It's an ideal bread to accompany savory dishes or to make delicious bruschetta.

 Preparation: **25 Min** / Rising: **3 h** / Cooking: **1 h**   Difficulty: **Low**   Serves: **4 people**

Ingredients

ALL-PURPOSE FLOUR	350 g (2 ⅘ cups)
WATER	210 ml (1 cup)
EXTRA VIRGIN OLIVE	30 g (2 tbsp)
DRY YEAST	5 g (⅓ tbsp)
SUGAR	1 tsp
SALT	1 tsp

for finishing

WATER

ALL-PURPOSE FLOUR

EXTRA VIRGIN OLIVE OIL

A little trick

To ensure your bread proofs perfectly, remember to **cover the dough** with a clean cotton cloth and place it somewhere warm, ideally with a temperature between 26–28°C/ 78–83°F.

Preparation

Combine the flour, yeast, and sugar in a large bowl. Pour in the olive oil, water and salt, then knead vigorously until a firm, supple dough forms.

Shape the dough into a ball, grease the surface with a little oil, then cover with a clean cloth and let it rise for at least 2 hours, or until doubled in volume.

Once the dough has doubled, roll it out with your hands (1). Roll it over itself (2), and roll it out again, repeating this process several times on both sides. Transfer the dough to a springform pan, cover it and let it rest for another hour.

Wet the surface of the dough with some water and sprinkle with a thin layer of flour. Make cuts with a knife (3) and bake in the oven at 180°C/355°F for about 60 minutes.

Remove from the oven, let it cool slightly, then serve.

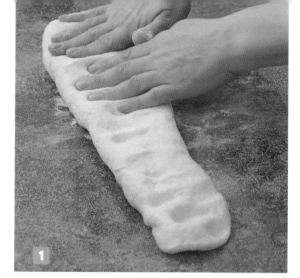

STRINGY CHEESE BREAD

Ultra-soft stringy cheese bread is a simple, incredible-tasting recipe. It's perfect as an appetizer served with cold cuts or as a hearty loaf of bread to accompany dinner. You can also offer it as a **delicious snack**. This cheese bread is perfect for any occasion!

Preparation: **35 Min** / Rising: **1 h and 20 Min** / Cooking: **25 Min** / Difficulty: **Medium** / Serves: **4–6 people**

Ingredients

for the dough

ALL-PURPOSE FLOUR	375 g (3 cups)
MILK, WARMED	180 ml (¾ cup)
CHEESE, GRATED	125 g (¾ cup)
BUTTER, MELTED	45 g (3 tbsp)
DRY YEAST	7 g (½ tbsp)
PARSLEY, CHOPPED	3 tbsp
SALT	1 tsp
EGG	1

for finishing

BUTTER	
EGG YOLK	1

A little trick

Use a chopstick to **flatten the center** of your strips of dough. It makes it easier to twist them.

Preparation

Combine the flour and yeast in a bowl. Add the milk, egg, butter, and salt, then knead until a firm, supple dough forms. Shape it into a ball, cover with a clean cloth, and let rise for 1 hour.

Divide the dough into four equal parts and roll each piece out with a rolling pin to form four rectangles. Brush the surface of each rectangle with butter and sprinkle with the grated cheese and chopped parsley.

Cover with a second rectangle, roll out the dough with a rolling pin and cut out several strips about 2 centimeters (1 inch) wide. Brush with more butter (**1**) and place the strips on top of each other, two by two. Roll them into a spiral (**2**) and continue until all the sheets are used.

Transfer the cheese bread to a baking tray lined with parchment paper, and let it rise for 20 minutes. Brush it with the egg yolk (**3**) and bake in the oven at 180°C/355°F for 25 minutes. Take the cheese bread out of the oven and let it cool slightly, then serve.

CIABATTA BREAD

Ciabatta bread is a **soft** and **tasty** bread prepared with a few simple ingredients; flour, water, yeast, and salt. Perfect for lunch or dinner, it also makes an ideal snack. Just add a drizzle of extra virgin olive oil and a pinch of salt.

Preparation: **30 Min** / Rising: **6 h** / Cooking: **15 Min**   Difficulty: **Low**   Serves: **4–6 people**

Ingredients

for the poolish

BREAD FLOUR	450 g (3 ½ cups)
WATER	450 ml (2 cups)
FRESH YEAST	10 g (¾ tbsp)

for the dough

BREAD FLOUR	300 g (2 ½ cups)
WATER	120 ml (½ cup)
SALT	15 g (1 tbsp)
EXTRA VIRGIN OLIVE OIL	

A little trick

To know if your dough has risen completely, do the **touch test**. Press the dough with the tip of your finger. If it bounces back slowly, it means the dough is ready to be baked.

Preparation

Dissolve the yeast in warm water. Add the flour and mix well. Cover with a cotton towel and let rise for 2 hours.

Once the poolish has risen, add water, flour, and salt and mix with a wooden spoon. Transfer the dough to a work surface, greased with a drizzle of extra virgin olive oil. Knead well until a firm, supple dough forms.

Place the dough in a lightly oiled bowl , cover, and let it rise for 2 hours. Turn the dough out, knead it briefly, and let it rest for another 2 hours.

Divide the dough into 3 equal pieces and shape each into a loaf. Transfer the loaves to 3 bread pans lined with parchment paper. Make small holes in the dough with your fingertips .

Bake the ciabatta on the lowest level of the oven at 270°C/520°F for 5 minutes, then place them on the middle shelf and bake at 220°C/430°F for 10 minutes. Remove from the oven and let them cool before serving.

ROSEMARY FOCACCIA BREAD

This fragrant focaccia bread is **crunchy on the outside** and **soft as a cloud on the inside**. How does it get this amazing texture? It's all thanks to the slow 12-hour leavening in the refrigerator. Indulgent and inviting, this focaccia bread is truly versatile and lends itself to any occasion.

Preparation: **25 Min** / Rising: **15 h** / Cooking: **30 Min**   Difficulty: **Low**   Serves: **4-6 people**

Ingredients

ALL-PURPOSE FLOUR	500 g (4 cups)
LUKEWARM WATER	400 ml (1 ¾ cup)
SALT	10 g (½ tsbp)
DRY YEAST	7 g (½ tsbp)
EXTRA VIRGIN OLIVE OIL	
ROSEMARY	

Preparation

In a large bowl, add the flour, yeast, water, and salt, mixing to combine. Knead until a smooth, supple dough forms.

Coat the dough with a drizzle of olive oil (**1**). Cover with a sheet of cling film, and let it rise in the refrigerator for 12 hours.

The next day, grease the pan with olive oil and roll the dough out inside the pan (**2**). Cover and let rise for another 3 hours.

Sprinkle the surface of the focaccia bread with more oil and make indentations with your fingertips (**3**). Sprinkle with rosemary and bake at 180°C/355°F for 30 minutes or until golden brown.

Once baked, take the focaccia bread out of the oven. Serve it hot or at room temperature.

A little trick

Did you know that brewer's yeast can be **frozen**? Just wrap it in cling film, or put it in a tightly sealed freezer bag, taking care to let all the air out first.

TURKISH BREAD

This delicious Turkish bread is cooked directly in a piping hot pan. In just 5 to 6 minutes, it puffs up, becoming **soft** and **airy**. Turkish bread is simple, versatile, and perfect for accompanying any meal, from breakfast to dinner.

 Preparation: **30 Min** / Rising: **1 h** / Cooking: **30 Min**   Difficulty: **Low**   Serves: **4–6 people**

Ingredients

- ALL-PURPOSE FLOUR   500 g (4 cups)
- MILK, WARMED   150 ml (⅔ cup)
- LUKEWARM WATER   150 ml (⅔ cup)
- SALT   1 tsp
- DRY YEAST   7 g (2 ¼ tsp)
- EXTRA VIRGIN OLIVE OIL
- CHOPPED PARSLEY
- CHILLI FLAKES

A little trick

To make Turkish bread puff up, remember to let it **rise well**, roll it out into as **thin** a sheet as possible, and cook it in a **hot pan**.

Preparation

Whisk the flour and yeast in a bowl. Stir in the water, milk, and mix to combine. Add 3 tablespoons of olive oil, then stir in the salt. Knead for 10 minutes, or until a supple dough forms.

Lightly coat the dough with olive oil, cover it with a clean cloth, and let it rise for about 1 hour. After it doubles in size, divide the dough into 6 balls and roll them out with a rolling pin to make thin sheets.

Heat a pan over medium–high heat. Place one sheet of dough into the hot pan and cook for 5–6 minutes, turning occasionally. Repeat with remaining sheets. Season the cooked bread with a drizzle of olive oil. Garnish with chopped parsley and chili flakes, and serve.

WATCH THE VIDEO

WE LOVE FRY-DAYS

How to fry perfectly: 7 tips for a flawless fried dish

Choose the right oil

Oils with high smoke points are best for frying. Two oils with high smoke points are peanut oil (230°C/446°F) and vegetable oil (230°C/446°F). The proper temperature for frying is 170–180°C/338–356°F, so high smoke point oils are the only types of oil you should use. Anything else can be harmful to your health.

Amount of food and oil

To avoid soiling the oil, fry food in small batches, about 100 g at most, especially if it has breading or batter.

Use a thermometer

The best purchase you can make if you want to fry well is a cooking thermometer. With this essential tool, you will always ensure that you are not beyond the smoke point.

Choose the right pan

Deep pans with high edges are ideal when it comes to frying. The most suitable ones are iron pans, but aluminum or copper pans are good alternatives. Steel is not recommended.

How to manage temperature

If you do not want the oil to burn, do not let it cook by itself. If the oil temperature starts rising, do not add more oil. Instead, add a little piece of bread to slow down the rate at which the oil's temperature rises.

When to add salt

Because of a physical process called osmosis, salt tends to pull water out of food. For this reason, if it's added before cooking, salt will moisten the outer layer of the food. This will make fried food less crispy. It's better to add it right after frying.

POTATO STICKS

Super **easy** to make and just **addictive**, this is the perfect appetizer idea to surprise your guests! So delicious and moist that you won't be able to stop at one.

WATCH THE VIDEO

CABBAGE ROLLS

Colorful and **tasty** cabbage rolls are a **delicious** second course to serve at any dinner or party. Cooking them twice makes them **soft on the inside** and **crunchy on the outside**. It's a simple dish that everyone will adore.

Preparation: **50 Min** / Cooking: **25 Min**   Difficulty: **Low**   Serves: **6–8 people**

Ingredients

CABBAGE	1
MINCED PORK	300 g (0.6 pounds)
SPRING ONION, DICED	1
GINGER ROOT, GRATED	1 piece
EGG	1
SOY SAUCE	2 tbsp
OYSTER SAUCE	2 tbsp
SALT	
CORNSTARCH	2 tbsp
SPICES TO TASTE	
VEGETABLE OIL	
ALL-PURPOSE FLOUR	

for the batter

ALL-PURPOSE FLOUR	
WATER	
SALT	
EGGS, BEATEN	2

A little trick

In this recipe, we used Savoy cabbage because of its large leaves and delicate taste, but you can also opt for green ot black kale. With black kale, your rolls will be smaller and thicker.

Preparation

Peel the leaves off the cabbage, wash them carefully, and blanch in boiling water for a few seconds. Drain, then place them in a bowl with cold water and ice.

Combine the minced pork with spring onion, ginger, and egg. Add salt, spices, cornstarch, soy sauce, and oyster sauce, then stir until the ingredients are well combined. Spoon the mixture into the center of each cabbage leaf and fold over to make many mini rolls (**1**). Place in a steamer and cook for 15 minutes.

Combine flour, water, and salt. Dip the rolls in the egg (**2**), then the flour, followed by the batter. Fry in oil (**3**), drain on a paper towel, and serve warm.

MEATBALL STUFFED POTATOES

This **unique**, **mouthwatering** recipe for potato boats stuffed with meatballs couldn't be any easier. Topped with melted cheese and seasoned with flavorful herbs and spices, this **tasty** dish has it all.

Preparation: **40 Min** / Cooking: **30 Min**   Difficulty: **Low**   Serves: **6 people**

Ingredients

GROUND MEAT	600 g (1 ⅓ lbs)
WATER	240 ml (1 cup)
POTATOES	5
GARLIC CLOVE, MINCED	1
ONION, DICED	1
EGG	1
PAPRIKA	
PARSLEY, DICED	
"PASTA FILATA" CHEESE	
CHERRY TOMATOES, HALVED	
VEGETABLE OIL	
SALT	
PEPPER	

A little trick

There is a perfect potato for every recipe. For this recipe, we suggest using **yellow potatoes**. They have firm flesh and are not too floury. Red potatoes are a great alternative if you don't have any yellow potatoes on hand.

Preparation

Peel the potatoes and cut them in half. Hollow them out with a small knife or a corer to shape them into boats . Fry the potatoes in oil until golden brown , drain on a paper towel, and season with salt.

Combine the ground meat, onion, garlic, egg, paprika, parsley, and breadcrumbs in a large bowl. Season with salt and pepper and shape the mixture into small meatballs.

Grate the cheese with a large-hole grater or cut it into thin strips. Put cheese inside each potato boat and place 3–4 meatballs on top. The number of meatballs may vary depending on the size of the potato boats.

Dilute the tomato paste with warm water and pour the sauce over the boats . Add some more cheese and a few cherry tomatoes. Bake at 180°C/355°F for 20 minutes, then remove from the oven and serve warm.

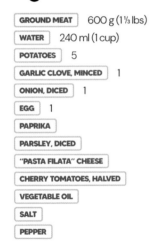

57

EGGPLANT FANS

Incredibly **tasty** but spectacularly **simple** to make, this delicious eggplant appetizer only requires a few ingredients. It will amaze your guests, and before you know it, there won't be a crumb left!

Preparation: **15 Min + rest time** / Cooking: **10 Min**   Difficult: **Low**   Serves: **4 people**

Ingredients

EGGPLANTS	2
EGGS	2
BREADCRUMBS	
VEGETABLE OIL	
SALT	
PEPPER	

Preparation

Wash the eggplants, then cut them in half. Slice the eggplant halves accordion-style with a sharp knife. Season with salt (**1**), rubbing it into the eggplant well, then allow it to rest in a colander for 15 minutes. Rinse and pat dry.

Beat the eggs with salt and pepper. Dip the eggplants in the eggs, then dredge them through the breadcrumbs (**2**).

Fry the eggplants in plenty of oil, flipping them from time to time. When golden brown, drain (**3**) and let dry on absorbent paper towels. Season with a pinch of salt, and serve.

A little trick

An alternative method for cleaning out the eggplants is to soak them in **water and rock salt**. Cover the eggplants with a plate and put a weight on them. A cup or a small pot works well. After 5 to 10 minutes, drain and rinse the eggplants. Doing this shortens the time needed for the procedure.

TOMATO FRITTERS

Soft, **airy**, and **delicious** tomato fritters are easy to make, and you don't need to wait for them to rise to achieve that cloud-like texture. This recipe is ideal for many occasions. Serve it as an appetizer course, at brunch, as a tasty snack, or even as a second course.

 Preparation: **20 Min** / Cooking: **15 Min**   Difficulty: **Low**   Serves: **4–6 people**

Ingredients

ALL-PURPOSE FLOUR	150 g (1 ¼ cups)
MILK	80 ml (⅓ cup)
PARMESAN, GRATED	50 g (4 tbsp)
PECORINO CHEESE, GRATED	50 g (4 tbsp)
BAKING POWDER	8 g (1 ¾ tsp)
EGGS	2
CHERRY TOMATOES	
SALT	
PEPPER	
BASIL	
VEGETABLE OIL	

Preparation

Beat the eggs with parmesan, pecorino, salt, and pepper. Add milk, flour, and yeast, and mix well until the batter is smooth.

Wash and dice the cherry tomatoes, then put them in a colander for at least ten minutes to drain excess water. Add to the egg mixture and whisk to combine.

Heat the oil in a large pan. Spoon the batter into the hot oil, and fry the fritters, occasionally flipping them until golden brown. Drain and let dry on a paper towel. Lightly season with salt, garnish with basil leaves, and serve immediately.

A little trick

If you don't have a thermometer and want to check the oil temperature, drop a breadcrumb into the pan. If it sinks, the oil isn't hot enough to fry. If it turns black, the oil has reached its smoke point, so you should throw it away. If the breadcrumb turns **golden brown** and it **starts to bubble**, the oil is ready for frying.

WATCH THE VIDEO

TORNADO POTATOES

Tornado potatoes are a **mouthwatering** side dish that is as **unique** as it is **delicious**. It's very easy to make and will be ready in just a few minutes. **Crispy**, **savory**, and **full of flavor**, everyone will love them.

 Preparation: **20 Min** / Cooking: **15 Min**   Difficulty: **Low**   Serves: **4 people**

Ingredients

MEDIUM POTATOES	4
WATER	120 ml (½ cup)
ALL-PURPOSE FLOUR	30 g
CORNSTARCH	230 g (1 ¾ cups)
PAPRIKA	1 tsp
PEANUT OIL	
SALT	
PEPPER	

Preparation

Insert a wooden skewer into the bottom of each potato, then push it all the way through the top, and cut them into spirals using a sharp knife. To make the spirals, start from one side and holding the knife at an angle, cut down in the opposite direction. Gently fan out the potato on the skewer, then immerse in cold water for at least half an hour.

Combine the flour, cornstarch, pepper, salt, paprika, and water in a bowl. Mix well. Dip the potatoes in the batter, letting excess batter drip off.

Fry the potatoes in warm oil until golden brown. When they are ready, remove from the oil using tongs, and drain them on paper towels. Serve warm.

A little trick

What should you do when your potatoes sprout? Potatoes that have recently sprouted are edible. Just **remove the sprout** and the surrounding area. However, if the sprout is **more than 1 cm long** or the affected area has a **greenish color**, you should get rid of the potatoes.

WATCH THE VIDEO

POTATO BREAD TRIANGLES

You can cook this easy potato bread in no time. **Super-soft** thanks to the potato dough, this dish is perfect both as an appetizer and served as a side dish with your main course. Potato bread triangles are a **tasty**, fast vegetarian recipe that everyone will appreciate.

 Preparation: **40 Min** / Cooking: **40 Min**   Difficulty: **Low**   Serves: **6-8 people**

Ingredients

POTATOES	500 g (1.1 lbs)
ALL-PURPOSE FLOUR	240 g (1 cup)
CHEESE	200 g (1 cup)
DRY INSTANT YEAST	10 g (2 ¼ tsp)
EXTRA VIRGIN OLIVE OIL	2 tbsp
SALT	1 tsp
PARSLEY, MINCED	1 sprig
EGG	1
PEPPER	
VEGETABLE OIL	

A little trick

Water in the oil usually causes splatter. To help prevent the oil from splattering while you're cooking, remember these helpful tips. **1)** Thoroughly pat all of the ingredients dry before frying; **2)** add a piece of unpeeled potato to the oil to absorb moisture; **3)** never cover the pot with the lid.

Preparation

Boil the potatoes, drain them, and peel while still warm. Smash them in a large bowl, and add olive oil, minced parsley, egg, salt, and pepper. Add the flour and yeast, then knead the ingredients until the dough is firm but soft.

Divide the dough into 4 parts and shape them into discs. Place 6 cheese slices on one disc, spreading them out like sun rays, then close with another disc. Make 3 long crossed cuts to form 6 triangles. Repeat with the remaining dough.

Heat plenty of oil in a large pan and fry the triangles, turning them halfway through. When golden brown, drain, let dry on absorbent kitchen paper and serve immediately.

WATCH THE VIDEO

READY IN 30
MINUTES

How to use a microwave to speed up recipes

Boiling potatoes

To save time, you can boil potatoes in the microwave. Put them in a microwave-safe pan, cover them with cling film and cook in the microwave at 750W for 13 minutes.

Steaming vegetables

Many vegetables can be cooked or precooked in the microwave. Chop the vegetables and place them on a baking tray with a little water, cover with cling film and cook at full power for 10 minutes.

Toasting dried fruit

Dried fruit can be quickly toasted in the microwave. Layer the dried fruit on a baking tray and set the microwave to full power. Cook for one minute, then check the fruit and mix if necessary. Cook for 20 or 30 seconds more as needed.

Preparing poached eggs

To make lightning-fast poached eggs, break the egg in a bowl and add water and vinegar. Cook in the microwave at 500-550W for one minute.

Soaking legumes

You can soak dried legumes faster, thanks to the microwave. Put the legumes in a large bowl with water and one teaspoon of baking soda, then set the microwave to full power. After approximately 15 minutes, shut off the microwave and let the legumes soak in the same water for 30 minutes more, then cook as usual.

CRISPY SMASHED POTATOES

Crisp and **golden on the outside** and **tender in the middle**, these amazing smashed potatoes are the side dish you need on your table right now! The most delicious and fun way to use up the bag of potatoes in your pantry.

WATCH THE VIDEO

MEAT SKEWERS IN BOTTLE

Here's a brilliant idea for preparing delicious meat skewers quickly and easily. With this clever trick, you can serve a **simple** but **tasty meal** and make your guests say, "wow!"

Preparation: **20 Min** / Cooking: **20 Min**   Difficulty: **Low**   Serves: **4 people**

Ingredients

GROUND MEAT	500 g (1 lb)
PARSLEY, MINCED	1 sprig
CHILI PEPPER, TO TASTE	
SWEET PAPRIKA	1 tsp
EXTRA VIRGIN OLIVE OIL	
SALT	
PEPPER	
MIXED SALAD	

You will also need

A PLASTIC BOTTLE

WOODEN SKEWERS

Preparation

In a large bowl, combine the ground meat, parsley, sweet paprika, and chili pepper. Add salt and pepper to taste and mix the ingredients (**1**).

Cut the plastic bottle in half, then transfer the mixed ingredients to the upper part of the bottle and cover with a glass (**2**). Put a wooden skewer through the opening of the bottle and squeeze it to form the meat skewers (**3**).

Place the meat skewers in a lightly oiled pan and cook on each side for 20 minutes (**4**). When they are well cooked, remove from heat and serve over a bed of mixed salad.

A little trick

Have you ever tried making **homemade paprika**? Cut a pepper into very thin slices, cook in the oven at 90-100°C/195-210°F and let dry for 5 to 6 hours. Grind the dried slices in a coffee grinder until you get a fine powder.

BURGER IN A HOLE

If you love **extra tasty burgers** and want to serve up something unique, this burger in a hole recipe is perfect for you. Just make a hole in the middle of the hamburger, place the egg in it, and there you have it!

 Preparation: **10 Min** / Cooking: **10–15 Min**   Difficulty: **Low**   Serves: **3 people**

Ingredients

GROUND MEAT	375 g (0.8 pounds)
EGGS	3
CHEESE (OF YOUR OWN CHOICE)	3 slices
HAMBURGER BUNS	3
EXTRA VIRGIN OLIVE OIL	
SALT	
PEPPER	

You will also need

GLASS   1

Preparation

Combine the ground meat, salt, pepper, and a little oil in a bowl. Shape your burgers and flatten them slightly with the help of a glass. Use the same glass to make a hole in the middle of each burger (1).

Preheat a non-stick griddle pan, grease it with a little oil, and cook the burgers over high heat. Place an egg in the middle of each burger (2).

Cook the burgers on both sides, then add a slice of cheese on top of each patty (3). Place the burgers in the buns along with your favorite condiments, then serve.

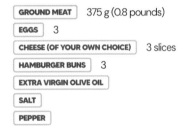

A little trick

Here are three tips for making the perfect hamburgers. **1)** Remove the burger meat from the fridge at least 40 minutes before cooking. **2)** Make sure that you always preheat the griddle or the pan before cooking the burgers. **3)** Salt the meat after removing them from the heat, and never while cooking.

BAKED
CABBAGE PIES

Cabbage pies with a **tasty baked egg filling** are an absolute delight. You only need a few ingredients to prepare this easy recipe. It's ideal as an **inviting** appetizer or as a **hearty**, **delicious** second course.

 Preparation: **15 Min** / Cooking: **25 Min**   Difficulty: **Low**   Serves: **4 people**

Ingredients

CABBAGE	1
EGGS	6
EXTRA VIRGIN OLIVE OIL	
SALT	
PEPPER	

Preparation

Remove the outer leaves of the cabbage, wash thoroughly, and blanch the whole cabbage in boiling water for 5 minutes (1). Drain and peel the leaves off the cabbage using a knife.

Put the leaves in a lightly oiled muffin tin, then crack one egg into each cup (2). Season with a pinch of salt and freshly ground pepper.

Close the cabbage leaves around the egg, being careful not to press too hard (3), and bake at 180°C/356°F for 20 minutes. Remove the pies from the oven and let them cool slightly. Unmold and serve.

A little trick

To break the eggs without shattering the shell, use a **flat surface** instead of the edge of a bowl.

POTATO TOAST

Potato toast is a **tasty** way to enjoy potatoes. It's a **simple** recipe that will amaze your friends and family. Everyone will love the **soft texture** and **wonderful flavor** of this easy-to-make dish.

 Preparation: **20 Min** / Cooking: **20 Min**   Difficulty: **Low**   Serves: **6 people**

Ingredients

POTATOES	750 g (1 ½ lb)
BREADCRUMBS	50 g (½ cup)
CHEESE CURDS	100 g (½ cup)
HAM	2 slices
EGG	1
ROSEMARY, MINCED	
EXTRA VIRGIN OLIVE OIL	
SALT	
PEPPER	

Preparation

Wash and poke small holes in the potatoes using a fork. Brush the potatoes with oil, and cook in a microwave at 700 watts for 6 to 8 minutes (depending on the size of the potatoes). Turn them halfway through the cooking time.

Remove from the microwave and peel and mash the potatoes. Place the mashed potatoes in a bowl. Beat in the egg, breadcrumbs, rosemary, and salt and pepper to taste.

Divide the mixture into small portions, shape them into squares and place them, one at a time, onto a sheet of parchment paper. Fill half the squares with a piece of ham and cheese, then cover with the remaining squares, pressing gently down the edges to seal.

Lightly oil the potato toasts and cook them on a well-heated griddle for 8 to 10 minutes, turning them halfway through. Remove from the griddle, cut diagonally to form triangles, and serve warm.

A little trick

To keep potatoes fresh for as long as possible, put them in a **paper bread bag** and store them in a cool, dry, dark place. The ideal storage temperature is between 4 to 10°C/39 to 50°F. It's best not to keep them in the fridge. Doing so can alter the potatoes' taste.

WATCH THE VIDEO

BAKED MEATBALLS WITH POTATOES

If you are looking for a tasty, satisfying second course, baked meatballs with potatoes is perfect for you. **Aesthetically pleasing** and **utterly delicious**, it is a **wonderful**, **appetizing**, **hearty** dinner.

 Preparation: **25 Min** / Cooking: **35 Min**   Difficulty: **Low**   Serves: **4 people**

Ingredients

GROUND MEAT	600 g (1⅓ cup)
POTATOES	600 g (1⅓ cup)
BREADCRUMBS	50 g (¼ cup)
GRATED PARMESAN, GRATED	50 g (¼ cup)
EGGS	2
GARLIC CLOVE, MINCED	1
PARSLEY, MINCED	1 sprig
NUTMEG, TO TASTE	
ROSEMARY, CHOPPED	1 sprig
EXTRA VIRGIN OLIVE OIL	
SALT	
PEPPER	

A little trick

If you want your meatballs to be softer with a more delicate flavor, replace the breadcrumbs with **stale bread soaked in milk**. Be sure to squeeze out the excess milk before using the bread for this recipe.

Preparation

Bring a pot of salted water to a boil. Add the potatoes and cook them for 5 minutes, or al dente. Drain and allow them to cool. Peel the potatoes then cut them into slices, and season with salt.

In a bowl, combine the ground meat, eggs, nutmeg, parsley, and garlic. Season with salt and pepper, and mix well. Add the parmesan.

Gradually add the breadcrumbs until the mixture is soft, moist but firm. Shape into small meatballs.

Lightly oil a baking tray. Line it with the sliced potatoes, arranging them along the bottom and around the edges. Place the meatballs on the bed of potatoes and divide them by putting a potato slice between each meatball in a vertical position. Season with a little more oil, sprinkle with extra parmesan and decorate with chopped rosemary.

Bake at 180°C/355°F for 20 minutes. Remove from the oven and serve warm.

WATCH THE VIDEO

RED LENTIL CREPES

This wonderful recipe has just two ingredients. Red lentil crepes are not only **soft**, **tasty**, and **light**, but they're also suitable for everyone, thanks to the fact they're **vegan** and **gluten-free**. Fill them with your favorite savory ingredients and serve them as appetizers or as part of a brunch spread. Everyone will love them!

 Preparation: **20 Min + soaking time** / Cooking: **15 Min**　　 Difficulty: **Low**　　 Serves: **2 people**

Ingredients

PEELED RED LENTILS	1 glass (1 cup)
WATER	2 glasses (2 cups)
EXTRA VIRGIN OLIVE OIL	
SALT	

A little trick

If you want your legumes to be **lighter**, let them soak in cold water with a tablespoon of baking soda. This will make them **easier to digest**. They'll also cook more quickly.

Preparation

Place the lentils in a bowl, cover in water and leave them to soak for at least 2 hours. Blend with an immersion mixer until smooth, creamy and without lumps, then add a pinch of salt.

Lightly oil a non-stick pan over medium heat. Pour 2 to 3 tablespoons of the batter into the pan and cook for 3 minutes or until bubbles begin to form on the surface of the crepe. Flip and cook on the other side.

Remove the crepe from the pan and transfer it onto a plate. Repeat the process with the remaining batter. Fill the crepes with your favorite ingredients, roll them and serve warm or at room temperature.

WATCH THE VIDEO

74

CAKE IT
EASY

How to replace eggs in sweet and savory doughs

Although egg yolks and whites might seem like an essential ingredient in the kitchen, you can **replace eggs** with several different ingredients. These easy substitutions work in sweet and savory recipes.

Bananas

Bananas - even ripe ones - are an excellent substitute for eggs. You can replace one whole egg with ½ banana.

Yogurt

Yogurt will make your dough soft and fluffy. Use ½ a yogurt pot as a substitute for each egg, both in savory and sweet recipes.

Potatoes

Potatoes are an excellent substitute for eggs in savory recipes. Use a medium-sized potato to replace each egg.

Milk

Both animal milk and plant-based milk can be used to replace eggs, especially for brioches or pound cakes. 50 ml of milk is equivalent to one egg.

Avocado

Avocado pulp has a texture similar to butter, and it has a mild flavor. It can be used in both sweet and savory recipes, using 1 tablespoon of avocado as a substitute for each egg.

Rice

Boiled rice can be used in savory preparations to replace eggs: 2 tablespoons of rice equal one egg.

Apple pulp

Apples contain pectin which is a powerful natural thickener. This makes it an excellent substitute for eggs in sweet recipes. Grate the pulp to remove excess liquid, and use 50 g to replace each egg.

TWICE
BAKED CAKE

A **soft delicious** cake with a **creamy filling** in the middle that won't sink to the bottom using this special trick. It'll be a family favorite for breakfast or snack time!

WATCH THE VIDEO

SPONGE DONUT CAKE

This two-tone cake is extremely **soft** and **easy** to make. Sponge donut cake is the ideal dessert for special occasions, holidays, or any time you're hosting friends and family. Everyone will love this **wonderful cake** - don't be surprised if it disappears quickly!

Preparation: **20 Min** / Cooking: **35 Min**   Difficulty: **Low**   Serves: **6 people**

Ingredients

ALL-PURPOSE FLOUR	300 g (2 ½ cups)
MILK	200 ml (1 cup)
SUGAR	100 g (½ cup)
VEGETABLE OIL	90 ml (⅓ cup)
UNSWEETENED COCOA POWDER	70 g (⅓ cup)
EGGS	3
BAKING POWDER	16 g (2 ¾ tsp)
VANILLA SUGAR	16 g (2 ¾ tsp)
SALT	½ tsp
WALNUT KERNELS	
CHOCOLATE CHIPS	

You will also need

| HIGH-TEMPERATURE RESISTANT GLASS | 1 |

A little trick

To prevent the nuts and the chocolate chips from sinking into the batter, **lightly flour them** before adding them. This will help them remain on the surface.

Preparation

In a large bowl, beat the eggs and salt with an electric mixer. Beat in the sugar and vanilla, followed by the oil, milk, baking powder, and flour. Mix until smooth and uniform (**1**).

Divide the batter into two bowls. Add cocoa powder to one of the bowls. Oil and flour a 22 cm (9-inch) cake pan, place the glass in the middle and pour the two batters into the pan at the same time, one at each end (**2**).

Add the chopped walnuts to the dark part and the chocolate chips to the light one (**3**). Cook at 180°C/356°F for 35 minutes. When ready, remove the pan from the oven and let cool for several minutes (**4**), then remove the cake from the pan and serve.

CLOUD CAKE

Indulgent and **soft cloud** cake is a delicious recipe inspired by master pastry chef Iginio Massari's yogurt pound cake. Cloud cake is a **quick dessert** you can customize according to your tastes. Enjoy it for breakfast or as a snack.

Preparation: **15 Min** / Cooking: **40 Min**   Difficulty: **Low**   Serves: **6 people**

Ingredients

ALL-PURPOSE FLOUR	300 g (2 ½ cups)
POWDERED SUGAR	200 g (1 ⅗ cups)
BUTTER	200 g (1 cup)
VANILLA YOGURT	150 g (⅔ cup)
POTATO STARCH	50 g (¼ cup)
BAKING POWDER	16 g (1 tbsp)
EGGS	5
SALT	1 pinch
VANILLA EXTRACT	2 tsp
FRESH STRAWBERRIES, TO GARNISH	
POWDERED SUGAR, TO GARNISH	

Preparation

Place all the ingredients into the bowl of a stand mixer. Beat for 4 minutes, or until the mixture is thick and lump-free (**1**).

Pour the batter into a 22 cm (8 inch) diameter cake pan lined with parchment paper (**2**). Alternatively, you can use a pound cake mold, as proposed by master Massari. Wash the strawberries, remove the stalk, and slice them into quarters. Arrange the strawberries on the surface of the batter (**3**).

Bake the cake in the oven at 180°C/355°F for 40 minutes. Remove the cake from the oven and let it cool to room temperature. Carefully remove the mold, sprinkle it with powdered sugar (**4**), slice, and serve.

A little trick

Do you want to prevent your cake from deflating in the center? Follow these 3 tips: **1)** Never open the oven halfway through cooking. **2)** Don't take it out of the oven right away, but let it rest in the oven with the door open for a few minutes first **3)** Don't exaggerate with the amount of yeast you add.

CHEESE AND VEGETABLE CAKE

Perfect as either a main course or a **tasty** side dish, this **savory** cheese and vegetable cake is super **simple** to make. If you're short on time or looking for an easy weeknight recipe, cheese and vegetable cake is exactly what you need. It's also ideal as a packed lunch or for a picnic.

Preparation: **30 Min** / Cooking: **35 Min**   Difficulty: **Low**   Serves: **4–6 people**

Ingredients

- **ALL-PURPOSE FLOUR** 400 g (1 ¼ cup plus 3 tbsp)
- **MILK** 150 ml (⅔ cup)
- **FETA CHEESE, DICED** 100 g (½ cup)
- **EXTRA VIRGIN OLIVE OIL** 100 ml (½ cup)
- **BAKING POWDER** 20 g (1 ⅓ tbsp)
- **EGGS** 4
- **GREEN CHILIES, DESEEDED AND DICED** 3
- **POTATOES, PEELED AND DICED** 2
- **TOMATOES, DICED** 2
- **SPRING ONIONS, DICED** 2
- **SALT**
- **GRATED CHEESE**

Preparation

Beat the eggs with a pinch of salt. Beat in the chilies, potatoes, tomatoes, and spring onions. Add feta cheese, milk, oil, flour, and baking powder to the egg mixture and stir well until the batter is smooth and lump-free.

Transfer the mixture into an oven pan and sprinkle grated cheese over the top . Bake at 180°C/ 356°F for approximately 35 minutes, or until golden brown. Remove from the oven, let cool, and serve .

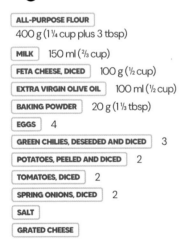

A little trick

Use the **toothpick test** to see when your cake is ready. Insert a toothpick into the center of the cake. If it comes out clean and crumb-free, remove your cake from the oven.

ONION CAKE

This isn't your average onion cake. It's a real **treat** with a rich texture and **mouthwatering flavor**. With our **easy** recipe, your onion cake will be not only soft and appetizing, but it'll also cook in no time at all.

Preparation: **40 Min** / Cooking: **30 Min**   Difficulty: **Low**   Serves: **4–6 people**

Ingredients

for the batter

EGGS	6
ALL-PURPOSE FLOUR	400 g (3 ¼ cups)
EXTRA VIRGIN OLIVE OIL	100 ml (½ cup)
MILK, WARMED	100 ml (⅓ cup)
BUTTER, MELTED	80 g (⅓ cup)
BAKING POWDER	20 g (4 tsp)
SOUR CREAM	2 tbsp
GRANULATED SUGAR	1 tsp
SPRING ONIONS, DICED	1 bunch
SALT	
PEPPER	

for the stuffing

CHEESE	300 g (1 ¼ cup)
BACON	250 g (1 cup)
LARGE ONIONS	3
CARAWAY SEEDS	½ tsp
VEGETABLE STOCK	300 ml (1 ¼ cup)

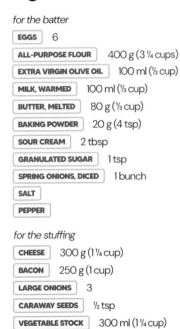

Preparation

Cut the onions into an accordion-style shape. Make cuts along the stalk and the sides of the onion, being careful not to cut them until the end. Bring vegetable stock to a boil (**1**). Add the caraway seeds and the onions and boil for 15 minutes.

In a large bowl, mix the eggs, milk, oil, and melted butter. Add the sour cream, flour, and yeast, then mix well until the mixture is uniform. Add the sugar, spring onions, salt, and pepper, and mix until smooth.

Remove the onions from the pot and fill each cut with a piece of bacon and a strip of cheese.

Grease a 24 cm (9-inch) springform pan and pour the mixture into it (**2**), evening it perfectly. Place and partially immerse the onions in the batter (**3**). Bake at 180°C, 355°F for approximately 30 minutes, or until golden brown. Remove from the oven, let cool for a few seconds, unmold and serve.

A little trick

Looking for easy ways not to cry while cutting onions? **1)** Use a sharp knife to slice through the onion; **2)** avoid cross cuts; **3)** soak the onion in cold water and vinegar for 5 minutes before cutting.

CHOCOLATE CHIP COOKIE CAKE

Chocolate chip cookie cake is a **simple**, **delicious** dessert that's perfect for beginner bakers. Similar to the crumb cake, this amazing dessert has the **tasty** addition of chocolate chips. You can make it with or without baking powder – either way, it's a wonderful treat!

Preparation: **25 Min** / Cooking: **30 Min**   Difficulty: **Low**   Serves: **6 people**

Ingredients

ALL-PURPOSE FLOUR	400 g (3 ¼ cups)
HAZELNUT CREAM	400 g (2 ½ cups)
CHOCOLATE CHIPS	150 g (¾ cup)
SUGAR	150 g (¾ cup)
BUTTER, CUT INTO CUBES	150 g (¾ cup)
EGGS	2
BAKING POWDER (OPTIONAL)	1 tsp
VANILLA EXTRACT	

A little trick

To make a perfect crumble cake, be careful **not to overwork the batter** and don't make it too compact. If you overheat the gluten, the cake will be hard and chewy instead of light and airy.

Preparation

Combine the flour, sugar, eggs, and vanilla extract in a large bowl. Add the butter and mix by hand until large crumbs form.

Add the chocolate chip and 1 level tsp of baking powder, if using. Baking powder will make the cake less crunchy, as well as taller and fluffier.

Press slightly more than half the flour mixture into a 24 cm (10-inch) cake pan, making sure to press the crumbs up the side of the pan so the base of the cake can hold the cream.

If the hazelnut cream is too thick, microwave it for 1 minute and then pour it over the base. Cover with the remaining flour mixture and bake at 180°C/356°F for approximately 30 minutes.

Once baked, remove the cake from the oven and let it stand for at least 10 minutes, then remove it from the cake pan and serve warm.

WATCH THE VIDEO

NO OVEN
NO CRY

Common misbeliefs about chocolate: 5 myths to debunk

Chocolate is a much-loved food that many of us enjoy from time to time. However, it is also the subject of plenty of misleading myths. Here are five **urban myths** about chocolate debunked.

Chocolate causes acne

Cocoa itself is not responsible for pimples, but some ingredients in chocolate like fats, sugar, and milk can cause acne. This is especially true of chocolate made with poor-quality ingredients.

Chocolate is addictive

Chocolate contains a small percentage of anandamide, an endocannabinoid with effects similar to cannabis. This is why some people wrongly believe it to be addictive. However, the amount is so small that you would need to eat 30 kg (66 lbs) of chocolate to develop an addiction.

Chocolate does not pair well with wine

According to expert sommeliers, high-quality chocolate goes very well with sweet wines and fortified wines, as well as with vermouth.

When white coating appears, chocolate has gone bad

Changes in the consistency of fats in the chocolate cause the white coating to appear. However, it does not mean the chocolate is spoiled. To avoid the white coating from forming, store your chocolate between 14 and 18°C/57 and 64°F.

High-quality chocolate is always dark

The quality of chocolate depends on the quality of the cocoa used to make it rather than the amount of cocoa in it.

BANANA ROLL-UPS

Easy, quick and **simply delicious**, these roll ups are one of the most incredible snack ideas that are loved by kids as well as adults. Just wrap the banana in the tortilla and make a tasty treat in a few minutes!

WATCH THE VIDEO

CHOCOLATE CUPS WITH COFFEE CREAM

These **tempting, crunchy edible** chocolate cups are filled with decadent coffee cream. Chocolate cups with coffee cream is a unique dessert that takes little time to make and calls for just a handful of ingredients: chocolate, coffee, and sugar.

Preparation: **1 h + rest time**   Difficulty: **Low**   Serves: **4 people**

Ingredients

ICE WATER	375 ml (1 ½ cup)
GRANULATED SUGAR	100 g (½ cup)
INSTANT COFFEE	40 (5 tsp)
DARK CHOCOLATE	
CHOCOLATE CHIP	

You will also need

PAPER CUPS

A little trick

To make the recipe even tastier, you can prepare an **espresso-flavored icing** to put on top. Pour a small coffee cup of espresso into a bowl and gradually beat in the icing sugar. The mixture should be smooth, creamy, and lump-free. When it is ready, place it in the fridge to set, then use it to decorate the chocolate coffee cups.

Preparation

Melt the dark chocolate in a bain-marie. Cut off the tops of the paper cups and pour the melted chocolate inside them (**1**). Make sure to fill them evenly, then let them set.

Repeat a second time to thicken the cups. Remove the paper cup from the chocolate cup. Use the melted chocolate to make the handles, then stick them to the cups with the help of more melted chocolate (**2**).

To make the coffee cream, combine instant coffee, ice water, and sugar in a bowl. Beat the mixture with an electric mixer until creamy (**3**). Fill the cups with the cream, garnish with chocolate chips (**4**) and serve.

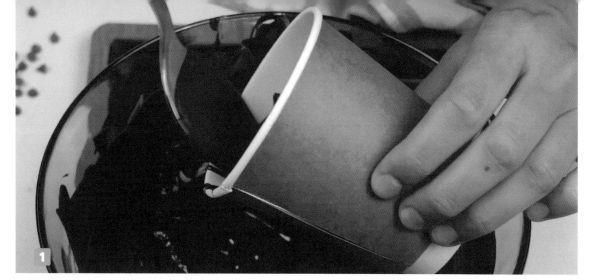

BANANA PANCAKE TACOS

With this **clever, delicious** banana pancake taco recipe, your pancakes will be **softer** than ever and even **tastier**. They get their amazing flavor thanks to the addition of the banana to the dough. They are meant to be enjoyed as small, sweet tacos and are simply irresistible.

Preparation: **10 Min + 30 Min of rest time** / Cooking: **10 Min**   Difficulty: **Low**   Serves: **4–6 people**

Ingredients

ALL-PURPOSE FLOUR	150 g (1 ¼ cups)
MILK	160 ml (⅔ cup)
VEGETABLE OIL	60 ml (4 tbsp)
GRANULATED SUGAR	30 g (2 tbsp)
WHITE WINE VINEGAR	15 ml (1 tbsp)
BAKING POWDER	8 g (1¾ tsp)
RIPE BANANAS	2
EGGS	2
VANILLA SUGAR	1 tsp
SALT	a pinch
HAZELNUT CREAM	

You will also need

| VEGETABLE OIL | 150 g (¼ cup) |

Preparation

Slice the bananas and place them in a kitchen mixer. Add the eggs (**1**), oil, milk, granulated sugar, vanilla sugar, and a pinch of salt, then blend all the ingredients until smooth (**2**).

Sift the flour and baking powder together in a bowl. Whisk to combine.

Pour the banana mixture into a large bowl and slowly add the flour mixture. Add the white wine vinegar, which will make your pancakes fluffy and soft, and keep mixing until smooth. Let rest for half an hour.

Lightly grease a pan with oil and heat over medium flame. Pour a few tablespoons of mixture into the pan and let it cook for a few minutes (**3**). When you see bubbles on the surface, flip the pancake and cook on the other side.

Once cooked, allow to cool slightly, then fill with the hazelnut cream. Fold in half, as you would do with tacos, and serve.

A little trick

Here is what to avoid to make perfect pancakes. **1)** Don't forget to let the batter rest for at least half an hour. **2)** Don't pour too much oil when greasing the pan. **3)** Don't go overboard with the number of fats in the mixture. Try and reduce it when possible.

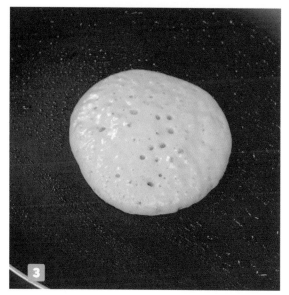

BISCUITS AND CREAM CAKE

Fresh and **fluffy**, this gorgeous cake will instantly impress your guests thanks to the **delightful decoration** alternating between biscuits, filling, and ladyfingers. Serve this for special occasions like holidays or birthday parties.

Preparation: **45 Min + rest time** / Cooking: **15 Min**   Difficulty: **Low**   Serves: **6–8 people**

Ingredients

for the base

CHOCOLATE-FLAVORED BISCUITS	32
LADYFINGERS	22
UNSWEETENED COCOA POWDER	2 tsp
MILK	200 ml (1 cup)

for the milk-flavored custard

MILK	1.4 l (6 cups)
GRANULATED SUGAR	200 g (1 cup)
ALL-PURPOSE FLOUR	60 g (½ cup)
CORNSTARCH	60 g (8 tbsp)
EGG	1
VANILLA EXTRACT	2 tsp
LEMON ZEST	

A little trick

There are two ways to fix curdled custard. 1) Slowly pour it through a fine mesh strainer until all the lumps are gone; 2) put it in a glass bottle, seal it well and shake it vigorously for a few minutes.

Preparation

Dip the ladyfingers in the milk and place them in a square cake pan, with the long side facing up. Alternate with chocolate-flavored biscuits .

For the custard: Heat the milk in a small pot, then add the sugar, flour, cornstarch, vanilla, lemon zest, and egg. Cook, stirring continuously with a whisk until the mixture thickens.

Pour the cream mixture over the ladyfingers , then over the rest of the surface. Cover with cling film and let cool in the fridge for at least 1 hour.

Remove the cake from the cake pan and place thin strips on the surface before sprinkling it with powdered cocoa. Gently remove the strips and let cool in the fridge for half an hour. Serve.

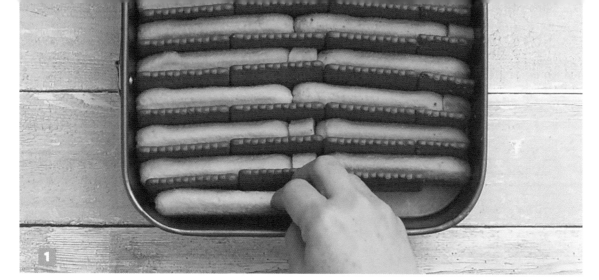

CHOCOLATE COCONUT YOGURT TRUFFLES

These **easy-to-make** chocolate truffles have a delicate yogurt and honey center. They're so **delicious** these truffles are sure to vanish from your table in no time. Coconut yogurt truffles are a simple, light dessert that you can prepare with just 4 ingredients.

 Preparation: **15 Min + rest time**

 Difficulty: **Low**

 Serves: **4–6 people**

Ingredients

- **GRATED COCONUT** 200 g (2 ½ cups)
- **NATURAL GREEK YOGURT** 150 g (½ cup)
- **HONEY** 1 tsp
- **CHOCOLATE**

Preparation

In a bowl, combine the Greek yogurt with the grated coconut. Add the honey and mix well. Shape the mixture into balls (**1**), then arrange them on a tray, and leave them in the fridge for at least 1 hour to set.

Melt the chocolate in a bain-marie. Spear the coconut balls with a wooden skewer and dip them into the chocolate (**2**). Leave the truffles to cool in the fridge for 10-15 minutes. Serve.

A little trick

Don't worry if you see a **white film on the surface** of the chocolate. It isn't harmful to your health. The white film is the fats surfacing as a result of heat and humidity. Once tempered, the chocolate will return to its original color.

WATCH THE VIDEO

CREAMY NO-BAKE CAKE

Creamy no-bake chocolate cake is the perfect dessert for chocolate lovers, as well as anyone who hates using the oven. It's a **delicious** and **creamy** chocolate cake that does not need baking. Ideal as a dessert, as a **tasty** snack, you can even enjoy it as a decadent breakfast.

 Preparation: **1 h + rest time**   Difficulty: **Low**   Serves: **6–8 people**

Ingredients

for the base

DRY BISCUITS, CRUMBLED	
350 g (2 ½ cups)	

GROUND WALNUT	150 g (½ cup)
BUTTER	250 g (1 cup)
FRESH CREAM	100 ml (½ cup)
DARK CHOCOLATE, CHOPPED	
100 g (½ cup)	

for the filling

| CREAM | 400 ml (1 ¾ cup) |
| DARK CHOCOLATE, CHOPPED | 300 g (1 ¼ cup) |

to decorate

| WHIPPED CREAM |

A little trick

The **ideal storage temperature** to preserve all the properties of chocolate is between 10 to 18°C/50 to 65°F, and never over 20°C/68°F. Store chocolate in the pantry. During the warmer months, keep it in the fridge or freezer.

Preparation

For the base: Melt the butter in a small pot, then add the cream and the dark chocolate. Cook until the mixture is smooth and uniform, stirring well.

Place the crumbled biscuits and ground walnuts in a bowl. Pour in the chocolate mixture and mix well. Transfer in a 24 cm (9-inch) cake mold and flatten the crust with the back of a spoon. Let it set in the fridge for at least 30 minutes.

For the filling: Heat the cream in a small pot. Add in the chocolate and stir until the chocolate melts. Pour the chocolate mixture into the cake mold and let it set in the fridge for 4 hours.
Remove the cake from the cake pan and decorate with swirls of whipped cream. Serve.

WATCH THE VIDEO

Thank you to the entire Cookist team that works every day with hunger, passion and dedication.
And to the publisher, Ciaopeople, that makes it happen.

WRITING
Francesca Fiore
Emanuela Bianconi
Jessica Matuozzo
Francesca Oppio

DESIGN
Sergio Esposito
Andrea De Luca
Alfredo Monzillo

PROJECT COORDINATION
Katia Valentino
Eva D'Onofrio

IN COLLABORATION WITH
Rossella Ferrigno
Giovanna Caso